How to Pray in Islam for Kids

A Comprehensive Guide to Performing and Understanding Islamic Salah and Wudu for Children

Table of Contents

Introduction

Have you ever wondered why your parents drop everything the minute they hear the Adhan and go for Salah? Have you noticed how they look more at peace after they finish praying Salah? Salah is a beautiful activity that brings you closer to Allah (SWT) and has the power to give you peace and make you a better and happier person.

This book contains all the information you need to understand Salah and how to perform it. It starts with an introduction to Salah and its significance in Islam. It then explains the meaning of worship and submission to Allah (SWT). You will also learn about the many spiritual benefits of Salah.

Before performing Salah, Muslims should perform Wudu to wash themselves. You will discover the significance of cleanliness in Islam and why it is an essential part of Salah. The book also explains how to perform Wudu like Prophet Muhammed (PBUH).

The book then moves on to the different positions of Salah. Have you ever asked yourself why your parents changed positions a few times while praying? Do you know there is a meaning behind each one? The book explains the different positions of Salah, their names in English and Arabic, and the correct way to perform each one.

Muslims pray Salah only after they hear the Adhan. The book explains the purpose of the Adhan, the meaning of each phrase, and its significance in Islam. You will also learn the time for each of the five prayers.

You have probably noticed how your parents always pray in the same direction. The book discusses the meaning of the Qibla, its role in Salah, and how to use a compass to find it.

Salah can change your life for the better. The book discusses the many advantages of performing Salah from a very young age. It then provides step-by-step instructions on how to pray.

Concentrating while praying isn't always easy, as your mind can easily wander off to other places. The book sets you up with interesting tips so you can remain focused when observing Salah.

The last chapter of the book focuses on Dua. You will learn simple Duas that you can repeat throughout the day, their benefits, and how to practice them every day.

This book has all the information you need to understand Salah and how to perform it. It includes the necessary instructions and tips to get you started.

Now, let's get started on this journey and learn about the power of Salah.

Chapter 1: What Is Salah (Prayer) In Islam?

Salah, or prayer, is a beautiful and fulfilling act. You speak to Allah (SWT) five times every day to connect with Him and strengthen your faith. It gives you the chance to be close to Allah (SWT) and ask Him for everything you want.

Salah has the power to ease your pain and sadness and fill your heart and soul with peace. When you are upset and you pray, you will feel as if something heavy has been lifted off your shoulders. Whatever negative feeling you have before you begin praying disappears in the presence of the Almighty (SWT)

Allah (SWT) doesn't need your prayers for He, the Almighty (SWT), has everything. It's the Muslims who desperately need it, as it can transform their lives and bring them rewards in the afterlife.

This chapter explains the significance of Salah in Islam, why you should pray from a young age, the spiritual benefits of Salah, and the meaning of worship and submission to Allah (SWT).

1. *Salah is a beautiful act. Source: chidioc, CC0, via Wikimedia Commons: https://commons.wikimedia.org/wiki/File:Muslim_Kid_Praying.jpg*

The Significance of Salah in Islam

Salah is one of the five pillars of Islam. One of the first commandments Allah (SWT) gave Prophet Muhammed (PBUH) was to perform Salah.

The Prophet (PBUH) said in a hadith, *"Islam is based upon five: the testimony of La Ilaha Illallah, and that Muhammad is the Messenger of Allah, the establishment of the Salah, giving the Zakah, fasting Ramadan, and performing Hajj."*

Allah (SWT) sent the Qur'an and all His commandments to Prophet Muhammed (PBUH) through the angel Jibreel (AS), except for the Salah. Allah (SWT) chose to directly tell His prophet about Salah and show its significance in Islam.

It is also mentioned over sixty-seven times in the Holy Qur'an.

There are other reasons that show why Salah is an integral part of Islam.

Worshiping Allah (SWT)

Muslims perform Salah to worship Allah (SWT) and ask for His help and guidance.

Allah (SWT) said in the Qur'an, *"O you who have believed, seek help through patience and prayer. Indeed, Allah is with the patient."*

Qur'an 2-153.

Every Muslim should have a relationship with Allah (SWT) since He is the one and only God. Praying five times a day can strengthen your faith in the Almighty (SWT) and bring you closer to Him.

"Indeed, I am Allah. There is no deity except Me, so worship Me and establish prayer for My remembrance."

Qur'an 20-14.

Protecting You from Bad Things

Everyone makes mistakes; no one is perfect. However, Salah can prevent you from doing bad things like lying or being cruel to people. It is so powerful that it acts as a shield to protect you from what Allah (SWT) has forbidden.

"Indeed, prayer prohibits immorality and wrongdoing, and the remembrance of Allah is greater. And Allah knows that which you do."

Qur'an 29-45.

Asking for Allah's (SWT) Forgiveness

Salah purifies you from your mistakes and any bad thing you might have done. For example, if you lied to your teacher about why you didn't do your homework, you can always pray and ask Allah (SWT) for His forgiveness.

Protecting You from Shaitan

Satan or Shaitan tries to make people do wrong things to anger Allah (SWT). However, Satan isn't as strong as you think. Performing Salah every day can make you more powerful than him, so you can resist him.

Getting Rewarded in the Afterlife

All Muslims want to go to heaven, right? You will be rewarded in this life and the afterlife when you perform Salah every day. Just imagine being in heaven and having everything you have ever dreamed of and more. How amazing is that?

"Indeed, those who believe and do righteous deeds and establish prayer and give zakah will have their reward with their Lord, and there will be no fear concerning them, nor will they grieve."

Qur'an 2-277.

Separating You from Non-Believers

One of the main things separating Muslims from non-Muslims is prayer.

Prophet Muhammed (PBUH) once said, *"Between faith and unbelief is abandoning the prayer."*

You perform Salah as a proud Muslim expressing your faith and love to the Almighty (SWT).

The Concepts of Worship and Submission to Allah (SWT)

You have probably heard the words worship and submission a few times when people talk about Islam. Worship, or as it's called in Arabic, "ibada," refers to all the things you do for Allah (SWT), like praying, fasting, reading the Qur'an, or giving money to the poor.

Do you know what the word submission means? Here is a hint: What religion are you following? Yes, submission means Islam. The whole religion is about submission or surrendering to the will of Allah (SWT).

However, submission doesn't mean you can't make your own choices. You can still choose to live the way you want, but you should obey the rules of Allah (SWT) and accept His will.

For instance, if something bad happens, you shouldn't say, "Why did this happen to me?" Or "Why is Allah (SWT) doing this to me?" It is OK to be upset, but you have to "submit" to the will of Allah (SWT) and accept that everything He does is for your good.

"Say, 'Indeed it is the guidance of Allah which is [true] guidance. And we have been commanded to submit to the Lord of all the worlds."

Quran 6-71.

When you truly worship Allah (SWT) and submit to His will, you follow His commands out of love instead of obligation. For example, some people treat Salah like a burden or something they want to finish fast so they can go back to playing. True Muslims love Salah and look forward to it every day. It is a welcomed break from all the noise and stress in their lives.

The Importance of Daily Prayers for Muslim Children

You are probably asking yourself, "Why should I start praying now?" or "Aren't I a little young to start praying?"

Prophet Muhammad (PBUH) said, *"Teach your child to pray when he becomes seven."* You are never too young to start praying. It is a beautiful and simple part of Islam that you should learn and practice from a young age.

Salah brings you peace and puts your heart and mind at ease. When you start praying from childhood, you will grow up to become a calmer and more relaxed person.

Muslims don't only worship Allah (SWT) by remembering Him or repeating supplications. There is a practical part of Islam that should become a part of their day-to-day lives, which is the Salah.

Salah shows you that your religion should be your number one priority. When you stop playing or anything you are doing to pray, you will learn that your whole life revolves around Allah (SWT).

Allah (SWT) has given you many blessings. Muslims should constantly thank Him for all His continuing gifts. The house you live in, your loving parents, the toys you play with, and your school (even though, at times, it doesn't seem like it) are all blessings you should be grateful for every day.

Praying teaches you gratitude from a very young age and gives you the opportunity to thank Allah (SWT) five times a day. There was no one more grateful to Allah (SWT), even during his worst times than Prophet Muhammed (PBUH).

The Prophet (PBUH) stood (in prayer at night) until his feet swelled up, and it was said to him: Allah has forgiven your past and future sins. He said: "Should I not be a thankful slave?"

Growing up isn't always going to be easy, therefore, you should develop a healthy habit of praying Salah and reaping its benefits whenever you face difficulties or are in a dilemma.

The Spiritual Benefits of Salah

You don't only pray with your body; every part of you joins in as well. Your heart, mind, and spirit all submit to Allah (SWT) and are at peace for these few minutes daily. There are many spiritual advantages to Salah that will make you understand why it should become a part of your daily routine.

You Stand Before Allah (SWT)

How many times have you had a difficult test or a bad day, and you wished you had a cool superpower that could make all your problems go away?

During the darkest of times, Salah can be a candle that lights your days. It gives you the chance to stand before Allah (SWT) and pray for anything you want.

Prophet Muhammed (PBUH) said, *"The closest that a servant is to his Lord is when he is in prostration."* Prostration is a position in praying that will be explained later in the book.

When you perform Salah, you are speaking directly to Allah (SWT). There is nothing and no one between you and Almighty (SWT), and you can say everything that is in your heart, knowing He is listening.

Prophet Muhammed (PBUH) said, *"Allah (SWT) continues to look upon His slave while he is praying, so long as he does not turn away."*

Although Allah (SWT) knows everything in your heart, speaking to Him will make all your problems and fears melt away because you have put them all in His hands.

Salah Calms Your Soul

Connecting with Allah (SWT) and constantly remembering Him through Salah can free your heart and mind from everything that stresses you out, making you feel calmer and lighter.

Gaining Positive Qualities

When you are close to Allah (SWT), you will be a better person and start acting in a way that will please Him. Salah teaches you humility and sincerity. You stand in the presence of Allah (SWT) every day, so you learn to be humble and sincere in everything you do and say because you know He sees what's in your heart.

Salah also connects you to your inner self or soul. You will learn to let go of your anger or ego and embrace compassion and empathy.

Salah Sets the Tone of Your Day

Pay attention to the way you start your day. If you wake up angry or upset, you will feel this way the rest of the day. However, waking up smiling and energetic will set a positive tone for the rest of the day.

Similarly, performing Salah first thing in the morning will give you inner strength and peace to face any difficulties throughout the day. You will believe that Allah (SWT) is always with you, protecting you from harm. You won't be worried or stressed, so you can focus on school or any other part of your life.

Prophet Muhammad (PBUH) said, "He who offers the dawn (Fajr) prayers will come under the Protection of Allah."

Making Better Decisions

Salah teaches you to always turn to Allah (SWT) with any problem you face. There is no one wiser than the Almighty (SWT). He loves you and wants to help you out; all you need to do is ask.

Salah also relaxes your soul, mind, and body so you can think clearly before making a decision.

There is nothing and no one in this world that can make you feel calmer or more at peace than Salah. It is no wonder that Prophet Muhammed (PBUH) and his companions spent hours every day praying without complaining.

Salah reminds you that Allah (SWT) is always watching you. You will think twice before doing anything haram or forbidden. Knowing that you will pray to Him five times every day will prevent you from doing anything that will make you ashamed.

Salah empowers you. When Allah (SWT) is always in your heart and mind, nothing and no one can ever touch you. Your faith becomes your strength, and you know that you can handle whatever life throws at you.

Prophet Muhammed (PBUH) performed Salah every day, and he loved it. Muslims of all ages should follow in his blessed footsteps. Don't wait until you grow up to start praying. It is easier to develop habits from childhood as they can remain with you for the rest of your life. Start praying now and enjoy the joy of connecting with Allah (SWT) multiple times every day.

Chapter 2: Wudu (Ablution) - Preparing for Prayer

Muslims should always be clean and take care of their hygiene. Prophet Muhammed (PBUH) was known for his cleanliness and nice scent. Before Salah, he would always take a shower and put on a lovely perfume.

Cleaning yourself before praying is both an obligation from Allah (SWT) and a sunnah. This activity is called Wudu or ablution, and it's more than just washing your body. You also purify your spirit, heart, and mind to prepare yourself for Salah.

Muslims must practice Wudu before praying, or Allah (SWT) won't accept their Salah. Prophet Muhammed (PBUH) said, *"No Salah is accepted without Wudu."*

This chapter focuses on Wudu and cleanliness in Islam.

The Importance of Cleanliness in Islam

Cleanliness is one of the most significant parts of Islam. The Muslim's body, heart, mind, and soul should always be clean and pure. No other religion has ever paid attention to hygiene like Islam.

"Truly, Allah loves those who turn to Him constantly, and He loves those who keep themselves pure and clean."

Qur'an 2-222.

Although staying clean and having good hygiene are nice qualities. However, in Islam, Muslims are encouraged to stick firmly to these qualities because it's important for their faith and how they live each day. Prophet Muhammed (PBUH) said, *"Cleanliness is half the faith ."*

Cleanliness isn't an option for Muslims but a must. Prophet Muhammed (PBUH) instructed his companions to take care of their hygiene. He showered all the time, kept his clothes clean, used a miswak (something similar to brushing his teeth), and disliked bad smells.

In the early days of Islam, Muslims took a bath every day before dawn to prepare themselves for the five prayers of the day. The Prophet's (PBUH) companion, Uthman bin Affan, bathed once, and sometimes twice, every day.

In Islam, worshiping Allah (SWT) is related to purity and cleanliness.

"In it [mosque] are men who love to clean and to purify themselves. And Allah loves those who make themselves clean and pure."

Qur'an 9-108.

One of the commandments Allah (SWT) gave Muslims was about cleanliness.

"Cleanse your garments and keep away from all pollution." Qur'an 74-4.

Cleaning your clothes is as significant as cleaning yourself. How can your body be clean if your clothes are dirty?

If your body, mind, and soul aren't clean, you can't connect with Allah (SWT) or perform Salah. This is why Wudu isn't optional but a must to worship Allah (SWT).

How to Perform Wudu?

Prophet Muhammed (PBUH) said, *"The key to the prayer is cleanliness; its beginning is Takbir (saying Allahu Akbar), and its ending is Salam (salutation)."*

Wudu has become a part of many ibada or worships. Muslims perform Wudu before Salah, reading the Qur'an, and performing Tawaf (a ritual Muslims practice during the Hajj).

You can't wash your body parts randomly. There are specific steps you must follow to practice Wudu.

"O believers! When you rise up for prayer, wash your faces and your hands up to the elbows, wipe your heads, and wash your feet to the ankles."

Qur'an 5-6.

Allah (SWT) mentioned in His Holy book the parts of the body that Muslims should wash during Wudu, but He didn't mention the order or how many times Muslims should wash each part.

Luckily, through Prophet Muhammed (PBUH) and his sunnah, Muslims know the proper way to perform Wudu. Girls and boys can practice Wudu in the same way.

Wudu Step-by-Step Instructions

1. Before you begin Wudu, set an intention, "niyah" in Arabic, that you want to purify your body to perform Salah. You don't have to say your intention out loud; it is enough to think about it and feel it in your heart. Just the thought that you are cleansing yourself for Salah or knowing in your heart why you are performing Wudu is enough. (However, if you forget to set an intention, it's fine. This is the only part about Wudu that is optional).

2. Think about your intention, "niyah" in Arabic. Source:
https://pixabay.com/vectors/brain-brainstorming-character-
smart-1773892/

2. Say Bismillah (in the name of Allah) once before you begin. Prophet Muhammed (PBUH) advised all Muslims to say Bismillah before they perform any good deed.

3. Say "Bismillah". Source:https://pixabay.com/vectors/talking-about-hug-joy-smiling-4824450/

3. Now, you will begin the Wudu. The first thing to do is wash your hands three times. The water should cover your whole hand and wash every part of it, including between the fingers, like in the picture.

4. Water should cover the whole hand. Source: Rasheedhrasheed, CC BY-SA 4.0 <https://creativecommons.org/licenses/by-sa/4.0>, via Wikimedia Commons: https://commons.wikimedia.org/wiki/File:Washing_hands_Corona.jpg

4. Next, rinse your mouth three times. Put water in your right hand (using your right hand is sunnah) and rinse your mouth. Don't swallow it. Leave it in your mouth for a couple of seconds, then spit it out in the sink and repeat two more times.

5. *Rinsing mouth using the right hand. Source: Ravi Kumar, CC BY 3.0 <https://creativecommons.org/licenses/by/3.0>, via Wikimedia Commons: https://commons.wikimedia.org/wiki/File:Mouthwash_(89914059).jpeg*

5. Then wash your nose three times, just like the illustrations. Take water in your right hand, sniff very little of it, then blow it out.

6. Take water into your nose with your right hand. Source: https://www.cdc.gov/parasites/naegleria/ritual-ablution.html

6. Wash your face, including your forehead and chin, three times.

7. Wash your face. Source: https://unsplash.com/photos/P6vDUuzL9Ow

7. Wash both arms, starting from the fingertips to the elbows, three times (wash the right arm first, then the left because it's sunnah).

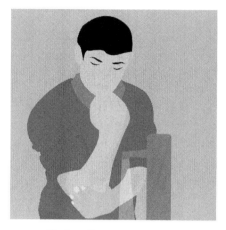

8. Washing arm till the elbow, starting with the right arm.
Source:
https://ar.wikihow.com/%D8%A7%D9%84%D9%88%D8%B6%D9%88%D8%A1

8. Put some water on your hands, then wipe your whole head.

9. Put some water on your hands, then wipe your whole head.
Source:
https://ar.wikihow.com/%D8%A7%D9%84%D9%88%D8%B6%D9%88%D8%A1

9. Using the same water, wipe both ears at the same time with your fingers once. (This part isn't a commandment from Allah (SWT) but a sunnah from Prophet Muhammed (PBUH)).

10. *Wipe both ears at the same time with your fingers once. Source: https://muslimhands.org.uk/latest/2018/05/how-to-perform-wudu*

10. The last part of the Wudu is washing each foot up to the ankle three times. Again, it is sunnah to start with the right foot. Use your hands to clean between your toes.

11. Wash each foot up to the ankle. Source:
https://unsplash.com/photos/4BSrd3e2Mjs

11. After you finish, say *"Ashadu an-la ilaha illallah,*
washadu anna Muhammadan abduhu wa rasuluh."

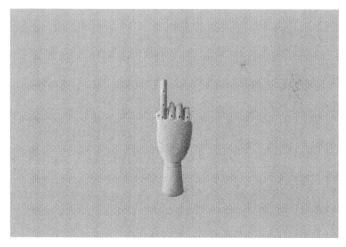

12. Say "Ashadu an-la ilaha illallah, washadu anna Muhammadan
abduhu wa rasuluh." Source:
https://unsplash.com/photos/YJxAy2p_ZJ4

You must follow every step, including the parts that are sunnah. Prophet Muhammed (PBUH) said, *"Whoever makes an ablution the way I have made and performs two raka'ah prayers in which he does not think anything for himself, his past sins will be forgiven."*

You can't perform Wudu in any other way or change the steps' order. For instance, you can't wash your arms before your face or only rinse your mouth once. Your Wudu won't be valid and your prayers won't be accepted.

After finishing the Wudu, dry the bathroom and clean it if there is any mess. Remember, good Muslims should keep themselves and their environment clean.

The Significance of Wudu before Salah

Would you attend a friend's birthday party in your pajamas and without taking a bath? Would you speak to your school principal with a dirty face or food stuck in your teeth? So how can a Muslim be in the presence of Allah (SWT), who is better than all other human beings with bad hygiene?

You practice Wudu because you love and respect Allah (SWT) and understand that you should be presentable when you pray to Him.

Wudu cleans your body from bacteria and microbes, protects it from diseases, and keeps you healthy. It also washes away dirt from many parts of your body so you can look clean and presentable when you stand before Allah (SWT).

Wudu also purifies your heart and soul as you set an intention to cleanse yourself from all the mistakes you have made. The water doesn't only wash away germs; it also washes away your bad deeds, so you perform Salah cleansed from the inside and the outside.

The Habit of Wudu before Every Prayer

If Wudu becomes a habit, prayer will be easier. Some Muslims don't pray when they go out because they aren't in a state of Wudu. For example, you are having lunch with your friends, and you hear the Asr prayer. All your friends go to pray except you because you aren't in a state of Wudu, and you don't like using public bathrooms.

Make it a habit to perform Wudu before you leave the house. Wudu is simple, and once you memorize all the steps, it will only take two minutes.

Allah (SWT) also blesses Muslims who are in a state of Wudu. Even if you aren't going to pray, perform Wudu so you can always be pure and blessed.

If you have an exam and you studied hard but are worried about it, perform Wudu before going to school. Trust that Allah (SWT) will bless you and make things easier for you.

Making Wudu and prayer a habit is easy.

- The moment you hear the words "Allahu Akbar," which are the call to prayer, go to the bathroom and practice Wudu right away.

- When you wake up in the morning, perform Wudu right after you brush your teeth.

- When you are going out, perform Wudu before getting dressed.

Allah (SWT) loves cleanliness. If you go back and read the verses of the Qur'an in this chapter, you will see that Allah (SWT) loves clean and pure Muslims. This shows the significance of cleanliness in Islam. Wudu is also a part of many types of worship, not just Salah.

Always be in a state of Wudu by making it a habit so you can pray anywhere and anytime.

Like Salah, Wudu also gives you inner peace and strengthens your spirit. It purifies your body and soul so you can be your best self when praying.

Remember, as a Muslim, you represent Islam and Prophet Muhammed (PBUH), so practice good hygiene and keep your body, face, teeth, hair, clothes, and environment clean. Make non-Muslims love Islam just by looking at you.

Chapter 3: Learning the Positions of Salah

During Salah, you communicate with Allah (SWT) using verses of the Qur'an, supplications, and certain body movements to express your love, gratitude, and respect for Him.

Prophet Muhammed (PBUH) said, *"When any one of you stands to pray, he is communicating with his Lord, so let him pay attention to how he speaks to Him."*

There are four positions in Salah,

- Standing

- Bowing

- Prostration

- Sitting

Each of these positions symbolizes Muslims' relationship with Allah (SWT). Standing up is a sign of your existence, bowing represents humility before Allah (SWT), and prostrating shows your admiration of Allah's (SWT) strength and power.

When you perform these positions, you feel humble and recognize the greatness of Allah (SWT). You are communicating your need and reliance on Him and that you are nothing without Him.

Muslims learned to pray by watching Prophet Muhammed (PBUH). He said in a hadith, *"Pray as you have seen me pray."*

Similar to Wudu, Salah positions aren't random. There is a reason and meaning behind each movement, which you will discover in this chapter.

The Different Positions of Salah

Muslims have to learn all the movements of Salah by heart. You shouldn't rush through the praying, but take your time and focus on each position and its purpose.

Prophet Muhammed (PBUH) taught Muslims how to pray through his sunnah and Hadith.

"Abu Huraira said: The Messenger of Allah (PBUH) entered the mosque, and a person also entered therein and offered prayer, and then came and paid salutation to the Messenger of Allah (PBUH). The Messenger of Allah (PBUH) returned his salutation and said: Go back and pray, for you have not offered the prayer. He again prayed as he had prayed before and came to the Apostle of Allah (PBUH) and saluted him.

The Messenger of Allah (PBUH) returned the salutation and said: Go back and say prayer, for you have not offered the prayer. This (act of repeating the prayer) was done three times. Upon this, the person said: By Him Who has sent you with Truth, whatever better I can do than this, please teach me.

He (the Holy Prophet PBUH) said: When you get up to pray, recite takbir, and then recite whatever you conveniently can from the Qur'an, then bow down and remain quiet in that position, then raise yourself and stand erect; then prostrate yourself and remain quiet in that attitude; then raise yourself and sit quietly; and do that throughout all your prayers."

Standing (Qiyam)

The first position you perform in Salah is standing, which is called "qiyam" in Arabic. Many things in nature are standing to praise and worship Allah (SWT), like the mountains and trees.

Muslims stand before Allah (SWT) with their bodies, hearts, spirits, and minds. Every part of them worships the Almighty (SWT).

While standing, your head should be bowed down with your eyes looking at the floor to show humility and that you don't carry any pride in your heart. You understand and accept that you are a simple human being and are in the presence of Allah (SWT).

The position with your head bowing down shows submission to the Merciful (SWT). For the next few minutes, every part of you will surrender to Him.

13. The first position you perform in Salah is "qiyam". Source: https://www.pexels.com/photo/photo-of-man-wearing-traditional-clothes-5988915/

Bowing (Ruku')

Bowing is called "ruku" in Arabic and is the second position after Qiyam. At this moment, you are like the angels in the sky who are constantly worshiping Allah (SWT) by bowing to Him.

All Allah's (SWT) creations, whether birds, animals, or plants, are always worshiping Him. Since animals are always on their four legs, Muslims bow in Salah to join them in worshiping the Almighty (SWT).

Bowing has always been a sign of respect, so, during Ruku', you are showing your admiration and submission to Allah (SWT).

You are also recognizing your place as a slave to Allah (SWT) while He is the Creator of the universe. You bow in hopes that Allah (SWT) will forgive you and answer your prayers.

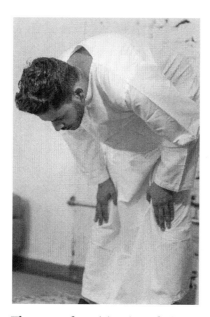

*14. The second position is Ruku'. Source:
https://www.pexels.com/photo/man-in-white-thobe-praying-
7129615/*

When you are standing, your mind is above your heart, but when you bow, they both come on the same level. This symbolizes faith where both the heart and mind are worshiping Allah (SWT) at the same time.

Prostration (Sujud)

Since the beginning of time, prostration, "sujud" in Arabic, has been a sign of respect. When Allah (SWT) created Prophet Adam (AS), He commanded all the angels to prostrate to him.

"And ʿrememberˋ when We said to the angels, "Prostrate before Adam," so they all did."

Qur'an 2-34.

This was a sign of respect to Prophet Adam (AS) and all human beings that Allah (SWT) created. Another interesting fact is that people used to greet each other with prostration until Islam came and prevented people from performing this position except for Allah (SWT).

Prophet Muhammed (PBUH) said, *"It is not appropriate for anyone to prostrate to anyone else."*

Prostrating is putting your forehead on the ground, as the picture shows. At this moment, you are in a state of complete submission to Allah (SWT). You can't see anything in front of you, yet you place your trust in Allah (SWT), recognizing that no harm can befall you in His divine presence.

You are giving your heart to the Almighty (SWT), and you have faith that He will always be there for you. No matter what happens in your life, you know that Allah (SWT) will never leave you alone.

At this moment, you feel that nothing else exists except for Allah (SWT). You are so focused and present and can pray and ask Allah (SWT) for anything you want.

Prophet Muhammed (PBUH) said, *"A slave becomes nearest to his Rabb (Lord) when he is in prostration. So, increase supplications in prostration."*

15. The third position is Sujud. Source: https://www.pexels.com/photo/man-in-blue-and-white-stripe-dress-shirt-bowing-down-on-red-and-blue-area-rug-7129384/

Sitting (Qa'da)

Sitting, "qa'da" in Arabic, is the last position of Salah, and it is just like the picture below. This takes place in the middle of the Salah and in the end. You are at peace while sitting and sending salutations to Allah (SWT) before you end the Salah.

16. The fourth position is Qa'da. Source:
https://www.pexels.com/photo/photo-of-man-kneeling-on-a-mat-5988919/

Activity #1

17. The 4 positions of Salah and space to write their names. Source:
Maqsoodshah01, Public domain, via Wikimedia Commons:
https://commons.wikimedia.org/wiki/File:Namaz-.jpg

Now that you have learned all the Salah positions, can you recognize them on your own? Name the right position under each picture.

Activity #2

1. Draw a Muslim praying and sitting.

2. Draw a Muslim prostrating.

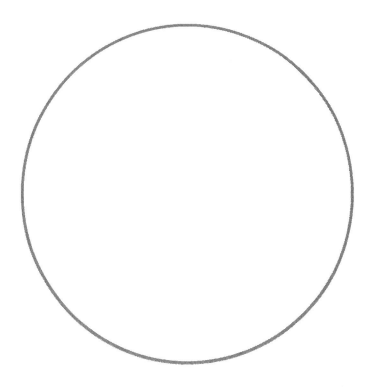

3. Draw a Muslim bowing.

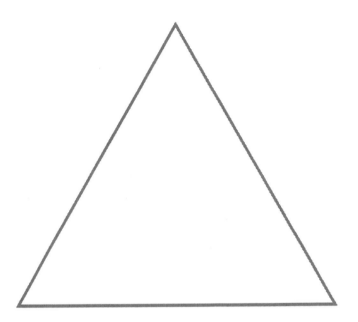

Praying is about performing specific positions to show your respect and submission to Allah (SWT). You don't only pray with your body but with your heart as well. Feel each position while performing it and observe how it gives you peace and gets you closer to Allah (SWT).

Chapter 4: The Adhan (Call to Prayer) And Iqamah

"Allahu Akbar, Allahu Akbar," are the first and last words in the Adhan or call to prayer. The sound of the Adhan and each word in it will make you calm and relaxed because they show the Greatness of Allah (SWT) and the beauty of Islam.

Adhan also reminds Muslims that they are about to embark on the magical journey of Salah.

Adhan is an Arabic word meaning "to listen" or "to announce." It takes place five times a day, and it always comes before Salah to announce to the Muslims that it is praying time.

So, what does the Adhan say? What is the meaning behind every word? What should Muslims do when they hear the Adhan? You will find the answers to these questions and more in this chapter.

The Story of the Adhan

Do you know how the Adhan came to be? There is an interesting story behind it. In Madina, Muslims used to wait at the mosque for Prophet Muhammed (PBUH) to come and announce the prayers.

In Mecca, people announced the Salah by saying, "The Salah is ready." However, as the number of Muslims was increasing fast, many people from different parts of the city couldn't hear the call.

Prophet Muhammed (PBUH) asked his companions to suggest a method to announce the Salah. Some suggested using a bell or a horn, while others thought lighting a fire or putting up a flag up a mountain for people to see from a distance was better. However, the Prophet (PBUH) didn't like any of these ideas.

One day, Prophet Muhammed (PBUH) was sitting in the mosque when one of his companions, Abdullah ibn Zaid, approached him looking happy.

The companion came to share his happiness with the Prophet (PBUH). Abdullah told him that he had a dream where he saw a man in green clothes carrying a bell. Abdullah asked the man if he could buy his bell to use to call the Muslims for Salah.

However, the man told him he would teach him something better. Then he said loudly, "Allahu Akbar, Allahu Akbar," and recited the Adhan for the first time to Abdullah.

Prophet Muhammed (PBUH) was pleased with this dream and knew this was a sign from Allah (SWT) that this should be the call to prayer for all Muslims. He taught the Adhan to a young boy called Bilal ibn Rabah because he had a beautiful voice.

Bilal climbed a high wall next to the mosque and said with a loud and beautiful voice, "Allahu Akbar, Allahu Akbar." His voice echoed all over Madinah, and Muslims came from every part, running to the mosque to answer the call to prayer. Interestingly, one of Prophet Muhammed's dear companions, Umar bin Al Khattab (RA), came to the mosque when he heard the Adhan and told the Prophet (PBUH) that he had the same dream as Abdullah.

According to hadith expert Bukhari, *"When the Muslims came to Medina, they, at first, used to have a time appointed for Salah at which they all gathered together, but as this arrangement was unsatisfactory, a consultation was held at which suggestions for ringing a bell or blowing a horn having been rejected, Umar (RA) proposed that a man should be appointed who should call out for prayer at which the Holy Prophet (PBUH) ordered Hazrat Bilal (RA) to call out for prayers in the words of Adhan as we now have it."*

Bilal was the first man in history to call people to prayer, and from that day, mosques from all over the world announced the Salah five times a day using the same words Abdullah saw in his dream.

18. *The Adhan calms people down and calls them to prayer. Source: Gentz, Wilhelm, CC BY-SA 2.5 <https://creativecommons.org/licenses/by-sa/2.5>, via Wikimedia Commons: https://commons.wikimedia.org/wiki/File:The_Muezzin%27s_Call _to_Prayer_(1878)_-_TIMEA.jpg*

The Meaning and Purpose of the Adhan and Iqamah

Can you imagine a world without Adhan? It would be dull and empty. Muslims need to hear the Adhan every day because it reminds them that Allah (SWT) is great; it literally says so in the Adhan.

Whenever you are sad or in a bad situation and feel that there is no way out, you can listen to Adhan. You will feel that Allah (SWT) is near you, and He will make all your problems go away.

The sound of the Adhan is also soothing and can calm you down whenever you are feeling angry or stressed. It is also so powerful that it drives Satan away.

The Prophet (PBUH) said, *"When the Adhan is pronounced, Satan takes to his heels and passes wind with noise during his flight in order not to hear the Adhan. When the Adhan is completed, he comes back and again takes to his heels when the Iqamah is pronounced, and after its completion, he returns again till he whispers into the heart of the person (to divert his attention from his prayer) and makes him remember things which he does not recall to his mind before the prayer and that causes him to forget how much he has prayed."*

If Adhan didn't exist and Abdullah never had this dream, how would Muslims know that it was time to pray? Do you think someone saying, "It is time for praying," will have the same effect on Muslims?

Adhan is a reminder to all Muslims that nothing matters more than Salah. Every word of it shows the greatness of Allah (SWT). The Adhan's main purpose is to let you know that the Almighty (SWT) is calling you, so you should run to Him.

The muezzin is the man who calls for the Salah. After the Adhan and right before praying, he also calls the Iqamah. The Iqamah is an Arabic word meaning "to serve" or "establish." "Iqamah Salah" means performing the Salah. It announces that the Salah is about to begin.

Prophet Muhammed (PBUH) said, *"When you hear the Iqamah, proceed to offer the prayer with calmness and solemnity and do not make haste. And pray whatever you are able to pray and complete whatever you have missed."*

The Iqamah is shorter and recited in a lower voice than the Adhan. The muezzin also pauses multiple times during the Adhan, unlike the Iqamah, which he recites faster. There is also a slight difference in the wording used in both.

Arabic Phrases in the Adhan

Have you ever wondered what is the meaning behind every word in the Adhan? Well, you are about to find out.

Allahu Akbar, Allahu Akbar (opening the Adhan), *Allahu Akbar, Allahu Akbar* (at the end of the Adhan)

Allah (SWT) is Great

Ash-hadu alla ilaha illa-llah, Ash-hadu alla ilaha illa-llah

I bear witness that there is none worthy of worship except Allah

Ashhadu anna Muhammadan Rasulullah, Ashhadu anna Muhammadan Rasulullah

I bear witness that Muhammad (PBUH) is the Messenger of Allah (SWT)

Hayya ala al-Salah, Hayya ala al-Salah

Hurry to prayer

Hayya ala al-Falah, Hayya ala al-Falah

Hurry to success

*As-Salatu khairun min an-naum, As-Salatu khairun min an-*naum (only in the Fajr prayer)

Prayer is better than sleep

Allahu Akbar, Allahu Akbar

Allah (SWT) is Great

La ilaha illallah

There is no god but Allah (SWT)

Further Explanation of the Adhan

The Adhan begins with an acknowledgment that Allah (SWT) is the Greatest. Next, it confesses the shahada, which is the first pillar of Islam and an admission of the Muslims' faith.

The shahada believes that Allah (SWT) is the one and only God, and there isn't any God but Him. It also confirms that Prophet Muhammed (PBUH) is His Messenger. The Adhan then calls to hurry to pray and succeed because Salah will bring you success in this world and the afterlife.

Each phrase of the Adhan is repeated twice to strengthen its meaning and get people's attention.

The Iqamah

Allahu Akbar, Allahu Akbar

Ashhadu alla Ilaha illallah

Ashhadu anna Muhammadan Rasulullah

Hayya 'alas-Salah

Hayya 'alal-Falah

Qad qamatis-Salatu, Qad qamatis-Salah (Salah is ready)

Allahu Akbar, Allahu Akbar

La Ilaha Illallah

The Significance of the Call to Prayer in Islam

You can't think of Islam or Salah without thinking of the Adhan. When Muslims anywhere in the world hear the Adhan, they know it is time to run to the mosque and pray.

The Adhan brings all Muslims together. The educated and the uneducated, the rich and the poor, the happy and the sad, and the grownups and the children become all equal. No one pays attention to their status as they all become just Muslims rushing to answer the call of their Creator (SWT). It is a beautiful way of showing that no matter who we are or where we come from, we come together as equals to pray and praise Allah (SWT) and we are all equal in the eyes of the Most Merciful Allah (SWT). Adhan has become a symbol of the presence of Muslims in any community. Many people have said that when they travel to a foreign country and hear the Adhan, they feel less alone. The call to prayer makes it clear that they are among friends. It brings Muslims together in the mosque, creating a sense of unity. If you can't hear the Adhan in a city or country, there aren't many Muslims in this place.

Adhan is a big part of every Muslim's life. Do you know that many parents recite the Adhan in their children's ears just after they are born? So, probably one of the first words you have ever heard was "Allahu Akbar." How great is that?

The Adhan sums up the messages of Islam. What is Islam about? It's about the oneness of Allah (SWT), Prophet Muhammed (PBUH) being His Prophet, rushing to prayer, and succeeding in this life and the afterlife.

All of these are repeated in the Adhan. It doesn't only call people to pray but also reminds them of the message of their religion. Imagine a thief going to steal something and, on their way, they hear the Adhan. They might feel guilty and regret their actions.

When Muslims are constantly reminded of the message of Islam, they think twice before doing anything against their religion that could anger Allah (SWT).

Responding to the Call and Preparing for Prayer

What should Muslims do when they hear the Adhan? They should drop everything they are doing and perform Salah. If you are playing or studying, take a break to answer the call of Allah (SWT). However, if you are in school, don't leave class and wait until after you finish, then go pray.

Remember, it isn't the muezzin calling you but Allah (SWT). Muslims should never keep the Almighty (SWT) waiting, as there is nothing more significant in life than worshiping Him.

When you hear the Adhan, you should silently repeat everything the muezzin is saying, except for Hayya 'alas-Salah, Hayya 'alal-Falah, you should say instead "'Lā hawla walā quwwata illa billāh'" meaning "there is no power and no strength except with Allah (SWT)."

Prophet Muhammed (PBUH) said, *"When the Muezzin says, 'Allahu akbar, Allahu akbar,' and one of you says 'Allahu akbar, Allahu akbar,' and then he says, 'Ash'hadu an lā ilāh illa Allah,' and you say, 'Ash'hadu an lā ilāh illa Allah,' and then he says, 'Ash'hadu anna Muhammadan rasūl Allah', and you say, 'Ash'hadu anna Muhammadan rasūl Allah', and then he says, 'Hayy 'ala as-Salah,' and you say, 'Lā hawla walā quwwata illa billāh,' and then he says,*

'Hayy 'ala al-falāh,' and you say, 'Lā hawla walā quwwata illa billāh,' and then he says, 'Allahu akbar, Allahu akbar', and you say, 'Allahu akbar, Allahu akbar', and then he says, 'lā ilāh illa Allah', and you say 'lā ilāh illa Allah' from his heart, he will enter Paradise.''

You can also make Dua and ask Allah (SWT) for anything you want between the Adhan and Iqamah, as this is a blessed time.

After you hear the Adhan, you should prepare yourself for prayer by following these simple steps.

1. Perform Wudu to cleanse your body and soul.

2. Go to the mosque to pray. Or, if you want to pray at home, spread a prayer rug in the direction of the Qibla. (The Qibla will be explained in the next chapter).

3. Set an intention and start praying.

When you hear the Adhan, listen carefully to each word and repeat after it. Feel it in your heart and notice the peace filling every part of you. Let the Adhan and its message make you proud to be a Muslim and grateful to be a part of this beautiful religion.

Chapter 5: Salah Times and the Prayer Compass (Qibla)

There are five prayers in Islam, and Muslims should perform each one at the right time. You should also pray facing a specific direction, which is called "Qibla." There is a reason Muslims perform Salah at specific times and a direction every day.

This chapter explains Salah's times, their significance, the Qibla, and how to find it.

Five Daily Prayer Times and Their Significance

Allah (SWT) said in the Holy Qur'an. *"And establish prayer at the two ends of the day and at the approach of the night. Indeed, good deeds do away with misdeeds. That is a reminder for those who remember."*

Qur' an 11-114.

Fajr Prayer

Fajr is the first of the five prayers, and it takes place at dawn and ends with the sun rising. It is usually dark outside during this time, but light follows later when the sun rises.

Muslims begin their day with the Fajr prayer, and observing it will set the tone for the rest of the day.

Dhuhr Prayer

The second prayer of the day is Dhuhr. It usually takes place at noon or midday, depending on where you live. The time of the Dhuhr ends at the time of the Asr prayer.

Muslims pray Dhuhr to remember Allah (SWT) in the middle of their busy day and ask for His help and guidance.

Asr Prayer

The third Adhan is the Asr, and it takes place after the Dhuhr ends, in the late afternoon. It ends right before the sunset, as Prophet Muhammed (PBUH) said, *"The time for 'Asr lasts until the sun turns orange."*

Maghrib Prayer

The Maghrib prayer takes place during sunset when the Asr ends. This prayer gives you the chance to remember Allah (SWT) before the end of the day.

Isha Prayer

The Isha prayer is the last Salah of the day and takes place at night, right after the Maghrib ends. It lasts till midnight.

You pray Isha to worship Allah (SWT) before you go to sleep and thank Him for His guidance and mercy.

The Significance of the Five Daily Prayers

Muslims pray five times a day to answer the call of Allah (SWT) and show their faith and love for their religion.

When Allah (SWT) first commanded Prophet Muhammed (PBUH) about Salah, there were fifty prayers a day. However, Prophet Muhammed (PBUH) pleaded with Allah (SWT) to reduce them because they would be too much for the Muslims.

Eventually, Allah (SWT) reduced it to five prayers, but they have the thawab or rewards of fifty prayers.

Prophet Muhammed (PBUH) said that Allah (SWT) said, *"I have enforced My obligation and made it light for my servants. He who prays these five prayers will be rewarded as if he had prayed fifty. What I decree cannot be changed."*

So why do Muslims pray at different times?

Nothing in Islam is random. Similar to Wudu and prayer positions, there is a purpose behind everything. Allah (SWT) chose the prayers at specific times for a reason.

If you look at the Salah times, you will notice they take place throughout the day at dawn, at noon, in the middle of the day, at sunset, and at night. This gives Muslims the chance to remember and worship Allah (SWT) all day.

You wake up in the morning thinking of Allah (SWT), you stop everything you do during the day to worship Him, and you remember Him at night before sleeping, all thanks to Salah.

The Qibla in Islam

Qibla is the direction all Muslims must face during the five prayers, which is the Kaaba in Mecca, the holiest place in Islam.

Muslims didn't always pray toward the Kaaba. Their first Qibla was Al Aqsa Mosque in Jerusalem. However, Prophet Muhammed (PBUH) had always wished that the direction of the Qibla would change toward the Kaaba.

The Prophet (PBUH) loved the Kaaba very much. When he lived in Mecca, he prayed, facing both Al Aqsa Mosque and the Kaaba.

This place is very special to all Muslims. Prophet Adam (AS) first built it, and Prophet Ibrahim (AS) and Prophet Ismael (AS) finished its construction.

"Surely the first House ˈof worshipˈ established for humanity is the one at Bakkah—a blessed sanctuary and a guide for ˈallˈ people." (Bakkah is Mecca, and this verse is about the Kaaba).

Qur'an 3-96.

The Prophet (PBUH) didn't disobey Allah (SWT) or even ask Him to change the Qibla. However, the Merciful (SWT) knew what was in His Messenger's heart. One day, Allah (SWT) revealed to His beloved Prophet that the Qibla changed to the direction of the Haram mosque where the Kaaba is located.

"We have been seeing you turning your face to the heavens. So, We will certainly assign to you a Qiblah that you would like. Now, turn your face in the direction of the Sacred Mosque (Al-Masjid-ul-Harām)." Qur'an 2-144.

Ever since that day, the Kaaba, also called Allah's (SWT) house, has become the Qibla for all Muslims. Five times a day, Muslims from different backgrounds, cultures, and races face the holiest place in Islam and perform Salah. Even if you pray alone, you know that at this moment, you are facing the same direction as millions of other Muslims from every corner of the earth. The Kaaba brings all Muslims together and unites them even if they aren't in the same place.

19. The Kaaba, also called Allah's (SWT) house, is the Qibla for all Muslims. Source: The original uploader was Medineli at English Wikipedia., CC0, via Wikimedia Commons: https://commons.wikimedia.org/wiki/File:Kaaba_at_night.jpg

For a few minutes each day, you are connected to the Kaaba, and your heart and spirit take a journey to this Holy place. No matter where you are, the Kaaba will be a part of you, even if you have never visited it.

Finding the Qibla Using a Prayer Compass

You don't have to live in Mecca, Saudi Arabia, to pray toward the Kaaba. You can face the Qibla from any part of the world. If you are at home, you can simply ask your parents or see the direction they pray toward.

However, if you are anywhere else, how will you find the Qibla? Don't worry, it is easier than you think.

Use a prayer compass and follow these steps to find the Qibla.

Instructions:

1. Find the direction to Mecca from your location by looking for it online or asking anyone in the area.

2. Hold the Qibla compass flat in your hand or put it on a table if available. The needle should be moving easily.

3. Wait until the pointer of the compass settles. This is the location of the Qibla.

20. Qibla compass shows where you should face to be facing the Kaaba.
Source: Maqivi, CC BY-SA 3.0
<https://creativecommons.org/licenses/by-sa/3.0>, via Wikimedia Commons:
https://commons.wikimedia.org/wiki/File:QiblaMat.jpg

The Importance of Praying at the Designated Times

Prophet Muhammed (PBUH) said, *"The best of the deeds in the eyes of Allah (SWT) are the Salawat (five daily Salah) in their prime times and after that, doing goodness to one's father and mother and after that, the best act is Jihad (struggle) in the way of Allah (SWT)."*

Muslims should perform Salah at specific times to get bigger thawab or rewards. When you drop everything to pray, you are showing Allah (SWT) that nothing and no one is more significant than Him.

You are prioritizing your religion and worship over things that won't benefit you in the afterlife, like playing, sleeping, talking to your friends, or just wasting time. You are also obeying Allah's (SWT) commands since performing Salah right after the Adhan is one of the best deeds in His eyes.

Salah is one of the most significant worships in Islam; if you don't perform it at the right time, you aren't taking it seriously. You don't consider it a priority, but something you can do when you have the time.

Prophet Muhammed (PBUH) warned against delaying the Salah as it could make Allah (SWT) angry. Salah is one of the most beloved worships to Allah (SWT), so don't let anything come between you and your prayers.

Nothing is more significant than praying on time. No one and nothing in this world should take priority over worshiping Allah (SWT). When you hear the Adhan, drop everything you are doing and perform Salah.

Memorize the time of the Salah and prepare yourself in advance so you are ready to pray right after the Adhan. It is significant that all Muslims pray at the proper time. Don't pray before the Adhan, as your Salah won't be accepted.

In severe situations, you can delay Salah, like if you are taking an exam. Other than that, make it a habit to pray right after the muezzin says, *"La ilaha illallah."*

Chapter 6: Practical Salah

Now that you know why Salah is one of the most significant parts of Islam let us get to the practical part of praying. Salah includes a few simple steps. Once you memorize and get used to them, you will be able to pray with ease.

This chapter explains Salah with step-by-step instructions, its benefits, and tips on how to stay focused while praying.

The Benefits of Salah for Kids

In many ways, Salah can change your life for the better and teach you great qualities that will benefit you in your childhood and when you grow up as well.

Discipline and Control

When you leave everything you are doing the moment you hear the Adhan to prepare for Salah five times a day, you learn to sacrifice your needs for Allah (SWT). During Salah, every part of your body is focused on worshiping Allah (SWT). If you make one wrong movement or say the wrong phrase, you will have to repeat the Salah. This teaches you discipline.

While performing Salah, you also learn certain movements and phrases that should be repeated exactly as they are. This teaches you to control your body and tongue for a few minutes every day.

In time, you will practice control and discipline in other parts of your life. For example, you will be able to control your tongue and prevent it from lying or saying anything haram or forbidden.

Makes You Active

If you pay attention to Salah's positions, you will notice they are similar to exercising. Practicing these movements multiple times each day can improve flexibility, strengthen your muscles, and keep you fit and healthy.

Bowing, or "ruku" in Arabic, improves your physical health and makes your back stronger. Prostration or sujud is very good for your brain's health; it can improve your memory and make it easier to concentrate on studies.

Prophet Muhammed (PBUH) said: *"If the people knew what (reward) there is in the 'Isha' prayer and fajr prayer, they would come even if they had to crawl."*

Refreshes Your Mind

When you practice Wudu, you wash your face and different body parts with water. If you feel tired or sleepy while doing your homework, doing Wudu will wake you up and make you feel refreshed.

Wudu and prayer will make you more alert and focused so you can pay attention to your school work.

Step-by-Step Instructions for Performing Salah

The steps of Salah are very simple, and you will get used to them fast.

1. Set an intention to only focus on Salah and worship.

2. Stand (practice Qiyam) and raise your hands to your ears, then practice Takbir by saying (Allahu Akbar).

3. For men, put your hand over your stomach, on your naval, and for women, place your hand on your chest. Make sure your right hand is on top of your left hand.

4. Your eyes should focus on the floor in the spot you will prostrate.

5. Recite Al-Fatihah, which is the first Surah or chapter of the Holy Qur'an.

6. After you finish, recite any other short Surah from the Qur'an that you have memorized.

7. Next, prepare yourself to bow down by saying *"Allahu Akbar"* and then perform ruku. Your back should be straight, your eyes should focus on the ground, and your hands placed on your knees. Repeat three times *"Subhanna Rabbeeyal adheem,"* meaning "How perfect is my Lord, the Magnificent."

8. Rise while saying, *"Samee Allahu leeman hameeda,"* meaning "Allah hears those who praise him."

9. As you stand upright, put your hands on your sides and say *"Rabbana walakal hamd,"* meaning "Our Lord, to You is all praise."

10. Before you prostrate or perform sujud, say *"Allahu Akbar,"* then prostrate. Your toes, knees, hands, nose,

and forehead should be touching the ground. Repeat three times *"Subhanna Rabbeeyal 'alaa,"* meaning "How perfect is my Lord, the Most High."

11. Say *"Allahu Akbar"* as you rise from sujud. Sit on your left foot, and your right foot should be upright, just like in the picture. Put your hands on your knees and ask Allah (SWT) for His forgiveness by saying *"Rabb ighfir li,"* meaning "Forgive me, Allah."

12. Perform sujud again and repeat *"subhanna rabbeeyal 'alaa"* three times.

13. Now you have finished the first raka'ah, good job! Repeat steps three to twelve for the second raka'ah.

14. Before you get up from the second raka'ah, you will perform the tashahud. Raise your index finger and repeat *"At-tahiyyatu lillahi was-salawatu wat-tayyibat, as-salamu 'alaika ayyuhan-Nabiyyu wa rahmatAllahi wa baraktuhu. As-salamu 'alaina wa 'ala 'ibad illahis-salihin, ashahdu an la illaha ill-Allah wa ashhadu anna Muhammadan 'abduhu wa rasuluhu"*

Translation: "All the compliments and prayers are for Allah (SWT), and all the prayers and all the good things (are for Allah SWT). Peace be upon you, O Prophet, and Allah's mercy and blessings. Peace be upon us and on the righteous worshipers of Allah (SWT). I bear witness that none has the right to be worshiped but Allah (SWT) and that Muhammad (PBUH) is His slave and Messenger."

15. Rise and perform the last two raka'ah. After you finish the last raka'ah, you will repeat the tashahud like the previous step and add a second part to it.

"Allahumma salli 'ala Muhammed wa 'ala aali Muhammed Kamaa salayta 'ala Ibrahim wa 'ala aali Ibrahim Innaka Hameedun Majeed Wa baarik 'ala Muhammed wa 'ala aali Muhammed Kamaa baarakta 'ala Ibraaheem wa 'ala aali Ibrahim Innaka Hameedun Majeed."

Translation: "O Allah, send prayers upon Prophet Muhammed (PBUH) and upon the family (or followers) of Prophet Muhammed (PBUH), Just as You sent prayers upon Prophet Ibrahim (AS) and the family (or followers) of Prophet Ibrahim (AS), Verily, you are full of Praise and Majesty. O Allah, bless Prophet Muhammed (PBUH) and the family (or followers) of Prophet Muhammed (PBUH) as You blessed Prophet Ibrahim (AS) and the family (or followers) of Prophet Ibrahim (AS). Verily, You are full of Praise and Majesty."

16. After finishing the second tashahud, perform the tasleem. Look to your right shoulder first and say, "Assalamu alaykum wa rahmatu Allah," meaning "May you be safe from evil, and Mercy of Allah be upon you" then look to your left shoulder and repeat the same phrase.

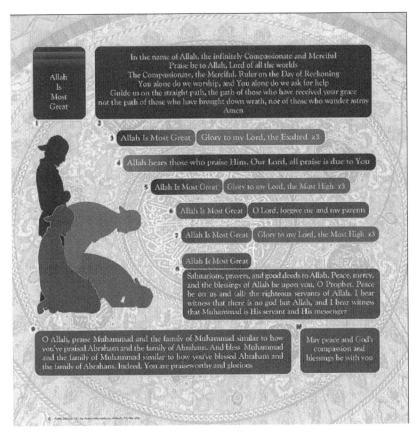

21. *All the steps of Salah that concludes one raka'ah. Source: Ayman Alhasan, CCo, via Wikimedia Commons: https://commons.wikimedia.org/wiki/File:Salat_or_Muslim_Pray ers_- _Illustration_showing_the_sequence_and_recitations_made_in_e ach_posture.jpg*

Further Explanation

This part explains some of the steps in Salah.

Setting an Intention (Niyyah)

Like Wudu, set an intention, or as it is called in Arabic, "niyyah" before every salah. You don't have to say it out loud; just keep it in your heart. Unlike all the other steps, you only do this step once, right before you begin praying.

The Opening (Takbir)

Muslims open the Salah with takbir, which is Arabic for "Allahu Akbar" or "Allah is Great." You usually do this by moving your hands like in the *picture,* as if tossing everything behind you so you can only focus on this moment and throw yourself in the mercy of Allah (SWT).

Takbir also gives you a couple of seconds to let go of all your thoughts and become aware that you are performing Salah. You no longer think of school, exams, toys, playing, or anything else.

Takbir also reminds you that you are standing in front of Allah (SWT), the Greatest, and there is no one in this world more worthy of your attention. When you say "Allahu Akbar," you feel calm and submit to Allah (SWT) to prepare yourself for worshiping Him.

How to Stay Focused On Salah

It is easy to lose focus and let your mind wander when praying. You may find yourself thinking about what you are going to eat for lunch or what you are going to do during the weekend. You shouldn't feel guilty for having these thoughts.

While you should only focus on Salah and not let yourself be distracted by anything other than worship, these thoughts aren't always in your control.

However, there are a few things you can do to avoid these thoughts so you can focus on Salah.

Avoid Distractions

Pray in a quiet room with zero distractions. Make sure to turn off the TV, put your phone on silent, and close the door.

It will be easier if you assign a space in your home just for prayer, like a corner in your bedroom or your parent's room.

Focus On One Spot

When praying, only focus on the spot where you prostrate to prevent your eyes from wandering. Just like you are in control of your mouth and body, control your eyes as well.

Pay Attention to What You Are Saying

There are beautiful meanings behind every Qur'anic verse you recite and every Dua you make while praying. Focus on what you are saying and feel every word in your heart.

Remind Yourself of Allah (SWT)

Whenever your mind wanders off, remind yourself that you are standing in the presence of Allah (SWT). Would you look away if you were standing in front of your school principal?

Allah (SWT) is Greater than any person in the world; He deserves your complete attention. Remember, He is the One who has blessed you with all the good things in your life. Express your love and gratitude to Him for a few minutes every day by giving Him your undivided attention.

Drink a Glass of Water

Drink a glass of water before Salah to improve your concentration. Thirst can also make it difficult to focus on prayer.

Change Qur'anic Verses and Dua

If you recite the same Qur'anic verses and supplications in every Salah, your brain will get used to them. You will repeat them without thinking and therefore, may struggle with concentrating.

Memorize different verses and Duas and recite new ones every once in a while. You can also open the Holy Qur'an and read from it while praying if you have trouble memorizing. This way, you will have to exert effort to focus on what you are reciting instead of repeating the same lines over and over.

Before praying, read their translation so that you are able to understand what you are saying. Recite every word slowly and take your time.

Don't Pray When You Are Tired

If you pray while feeling tired, you will be easily distracted and, in a hurry to finish. Although you shouldn't delay prayer, it is OK if you take a few minutes to rest and regain your energy before praying.

You can jump up and down to energize yourself. Breathing exercises are also helpful as they can make you alert and relaxed.

Breathing Exercise

1. Sit on a comfortable chair.

2. Take a long, deep breath through your nose until your belly is filled with air.

3. Breathe out through your mouth while making a "Ha" noise.

4. Repeat until you feel energetic.

Ali bin Abi Talib (RA) was Prophet Muhammed's (PBUH) beloved cousin and companion. He once said, *"None of you should ever stand for Prayer in a lazy or drowsy state."*

Don't Delay Prayer

If you aren't tired, don't delay your prayer. The more you wait, the more it will feel like a burden and chore to be completed, and you will struggle with staying focused.

Salah isn't a marathon. Don't rush yourself to get to the finish line. Enjoy the experience and understand that you are worshiping Allah (SWT), the creator of the world! Give it the time and attention it deserves.

Performing Salah is easy. Although it includes many steps, you will soon get used to them. Do you see how your parents pray without any instructions? You will, too.

Salah is a lot simpler than you think. The more you perform it, the easier it will get.

Chapter 7: Daily Duas (Supplications) for Kids

Dua or supplication is asking Allah (SWT) for anything you need, whether it is something big like doing well in your exam or small like your parents buying you a new toy. Dua gives you the chance to constantly communicate with Allah (SWT) and be close to Him.

22. *Dua gives you the chance to constantly communicate with Allah (SWT) and be close to Him. Source: kiiofficial, CC BY-SA 4.0 <https://creativecommons.org/licenses/by-sa/4.0>, via Wikimedia Commons: https://commons.wikimedia.org/wiki/File:Duaa.jpg*

You can practice supplications anytime and anywhere during the day. You don't have to be in a state of Wudu or face the Qibla. You can even make Dua with your heart if you are in a public place.

Allah (SWT) wants Muslims to ask Him for anything they want. In many verses of the Qur'an, He encourages them to always pray to him.

"When my servants ask you concerning me, (tell them) I am indeed close (to them). I listen to the prayer of every suppliant when he calls on me."

Qur'an 2-186.

Dua is also a type of worship, and you will get rewards for practicing it.

Prophet Muhammed (PBUH) said, *"The most excellent worship is Dua."*

The essence of the Dua is understanding that you are weak and recognizing the power of Allah (SWT). You are completely submissive to Him, and you acknowledge your need for His forgiveness, mercy, and generosity.

In this chapter, you will learn simple Duas you can practice every day and their meanings.

O Allah, increase me in knowledge.

Dua before Sleeping

Recite this Dua before your sleep like Prophet Muhammed (PBUH) did. Ask Allah (SWT) to sleep and awake with His name and remembrance.

اللَّهُمَّ بِاسْمِكَ أَمُوتُ وَأَحْيَا

In Your name O Allah, I live and die

Dua after Waking up

Prophet Muhammed (PBUH) recited this Dua after waking up to thank Allah (SWT) that he got up after sleeping. It is a beautiful Dua to repeat to show your gratitude to Allah (SWT) for a new day.

اَلْحَمْدُ لِلَّهِ الَّذي أَحْيَانَا بَعْدَ ‏١ مَا‏١ اَمَاتَنَا وَإِلَيْهِ النُّشُورُ.

All praise is for Allah who gave us life after having taken it from us, and unto Him is the resurrection.

Dua before Eating

Before you eat, ask Allah (SWT) to bless your food.

اَللَّهُمَّ بَارِ ‏١ لَنَا فِيهِ وَأَطعِمنَا خَيرَ أَ‏١نه

O Allah, bless it for us and feed us better than it.

Dua after Eating

Food is a blessing that many people don't have. Express your gratitude to Allah (SWT) every day after eating to thank Him for the gifts that you wouldn't have been able to receive without His generosity.

الْحَمْدُ لِلهِ حَمْداً كَثِيراً طَيّباً ‏١ بَارَكاً فيه غَيْرَ‏١كُفِيّ وَلاَ ‏١ وَدَّعٍ وَلاَ ‏١ سْتَغْنىً عَنْهُ رَبَّنَا

Allah be praised with abundant, beautiful, blessed praise. He is The One Who is sufficient, feeds, and is not fed. The One Who is longed for, along with that which is with Him and The One Who is needed, He is our Lord. Allah be praised.

If this Dua is too long for you, you can just say *"alhamdulillah"* or "Allah be praised" after every meal.

Dua after Drinking Milk

Prophet Muhammed (PBUH) recited this Dua after drinking milk. You can also recite it before drinking water to ask for Allah's (SWT) blessings.

اللّٰهُمَّ بَارِ؟ لَنَا فِيهِ وَزِدْنَا؟نْه

Allah bless us in it and grant us more

Dua before Going to the Bathroom and after Getting Out

The bathroom is a dirty place, so ask for Allah's (SWT) protection before you get in and forgiveness when you get out.

Dua before Going to the Bathroom

بِسْمِ اللَّٰهِ. اللَّهُمَّ إِنِّي أَعُوذُ بِكَ؟نَ الْخُبْثِ وَالْخَبَائِثِ

In the name of Allah, O Allah, I take refuge in you from evil and evil-doers.

Dua after Getting out of the Bathroom

غُفْرَانَكَ

I ask You for forgiveness, oh Allah.

Dua before Wearing Clothes

Many people aren't blessed like you. Remember to thank Allah (SWT) every time you get dressed because He chose to bless you with the gift of clothes and luxury.

You are also declaring that Allah (SWT) is the one who provided these clothes for you and that you owe everything to Him.

.ٱلْحَمْدُ لِلَّهِ الَّذِي كَسَانِي هَذَا (الثَّوْبَ) وَرَزَقَنِيهِ؟نْ غَيْرِ حَوْلٍ؟نِّي وَلَا قُوَّةٍ

All Praise is for Allah, who has clothed me with this garment and provided it for me, with no power or might from myself.

Dua before Leaving Home

Before leaving the house, make this Dua to ask for Allah's (SWT) guidance and protection until you get home.

بِسْمِ اللَّهِ تَوَكَّلْتُ عَلَى اللَّهِ، وَلاَ حَوْلَ وَلاَ قُوَّةَ إِلاَّ بِاللَّهِ.

In the name of Allah, I place my trust in Allah, and there is no might nor power except with Allah.

Dua When Riding Transportation

Thank Allah (SWT) when getting on the bus, your parent's car, or any other method of transportation. You may not realize it, but cars, buses, etc., make your life easier, and they are a blessing from Allah (SWT).

Although Prophet Muhammed (PBUH) didn't have a car, he repeated this Dua whenever he mounted a camel or horse, as this was the method of transportation back in the day.

بِسْمِ اللهِ وَالْحَمْدُ لله سُبْحَانَ الَّذِي سَخَّرَ لَنَا هَذَا وَمَا كُنَّا لَهُ مُقْرِنِينَ * وَإِنَّا إِلَى رَبِّنَا لَمُنقَلِبُونَ الْحَمْدُ لله الْحَمْدُ لله الْحَمْدُ لله اللهُ أَكْبَرُ اللهُ أَكْبَرُ اللهُ أَكْبَرُ سُبْحَانَكَ اللَّهُمَّ إِنِّي ظَلَمْتُ نَفْسِي فَاغْفِرْ لِي فَإِنَّهُ لا يَغْفِرُ الذُّنُوبَ إِلاَّ أَنْتَ

In the name of Allah, all praise is for Allah. How perfect He is, the One Who has placed this (transport) at our service, and we ourselves would not have been capable of that, and to our Lord is our final destiny. All praise is for Allah, All praise is for Allah, All praise is for Allah, Allah is the greatest, Allah is the greatest, Allah is the greatest. How perfect You are, O Allah, verily I have wronged my soul, so forgive me, for surely none can forgive sins except You.

Dua When Entering Home

Recite this Dua after you get home to have Allah's (SWT) blessings with you when you enter your house.

بِسْمِ اللهِ وَلَجْنَا، وَبِسْمِ اللهِ خَرَجْنَا، وَعَلَى رَبِّنَا تَوَكَّلْنَا.

In the name of Allah, we enter, and in the name of Allah, we leave, and upon our Lord, we place our trust.

Dua for Increasing Knowledge

Prophet Muhammed (PBUH) made this Dua after praying al-Fajr to ask Allah (SWT) to increase his knowledge.

اللهم إني أسألك علماً نافعاً، ورزقاً طيباً، وعملاً تقبلاً

O Allah, indeed, I ask You for beneficial knowledge, a good Halal provision, and actions that are accepted

Make this Dua before studying so you can benefit from everything you are learning.

This is also another great Dua to repeat before studying.

رَّبِّ زِدْنِي عِلْمًا

O Allah, increase my knowledge.

Most of these Duas are to remember and thank Allah (SWT). Expressing your gratitude to Allah (SWT) will increase your blessings and happiness.

Allah (SWT) said, *"If you are grateful, I will certainly give you more."*

Qur'an 14-7.

How to Make Dua a Part of Your Daily Routine

There are simple things that you can do to remember reciting these Duas.

- Write them on sticky notes and hang them around the house. For example, you can hang the sleep and wake-up Duas in your bedroom.

- Start with simple supplications by memorizing one or two Duas, and once you get used to reciting them at the appropriate time, memorize another two.

- Don't go a day without reciting Duas, even if it is just one. In time, it will become a habit.

- Keep Allah (SWT) on your mind throughout the day so that when you are about to eat or drink, you will remember the Duas.

- Get a calendar and write down the days you remembered to recite all the Duas. This way, you will track your progress and motivate yourself to keep going.

You need to practice supplications because they will bring you blessings and will improve your life in different ways. Allah (SWT) loves hearing the voice of His worshipers and will certainly bless you in different ways when you ask Him.

He may not give you exactly what you want every time, but you will always receive great things from Him, even when you aren't aware of it.

Conclusion

Now, do you understand why your parents make praying their priority? Salah is a relaxing activity that only takes a few minutes to complete every day. It will make you feel at peace and can be a pleasant break from the hectic routine or anything that makes you stressed or sad.

The book began by explaining in detail what Salah is and why every Muslim should perform it every day. It also covered how Salah is one of the pillars of Islam and how it's a main part of worship and submission to Allah (SWT). You also learned the effect of daily prayers on your heart and spirit.

Muslims should always be clean and put together. The book stresses the significance of wudu and why cleanliness is a major part of Islam. It also illustrated how to perform wudu in simple steps.

Performing each position in Salah correctly is of utmost significance, so Allah (SWT) will accept your prayers. The book provided a detailed explanation of each position and instructions on how to perform them. The call to prayer is beautiful and peaceful, even if you don't understand what it means. The book explains its meaning and purpose and how to respond to each word. It also provided verses from the Qur'an and different Hadiths to highlight the purpose and significance of the Adhan.

The book discussed the number of times Muslims should perform Salah and why they should pray on time. It also explained the concept of Qibla and the direction all Muslims must face while praying. It also described how to use a compass to find the Qibla in any place.

All Muslims should start praying when they turn seven. Performing Salah at a young age can teach you discipline and encourage you to be connected with Allah (SWT). The book discussed the many benefits of Salah and how it builds character.

The book then moved to the practical part and provided instructions on how to perform every part of Salah. It also gave you effective advice to concentrate for a few minutes on the act of praying.

Allah (SWT) wants His worshipers to ask for anything they want and to constantly pray for His forgiveness. The book explained the power of Dua and offered examples of Prophet Muhammed's (PBUH) favorite Duas.

Salah is not only the physical movement of your body, it is a journey that connects the believer to the Divine. Salah can change your heart and soul, so give it a chance to transform your life.

References

5 Practical tips to increase focus in Salah - Understand Al-Qur'an Academy. (2017, May 25). Understand Al-Qur'an Academy. https://understandquran.com/5-practical-tips-increase-focus-salah/

5 spiritual impacts of Salah in our daily lives. (n.d.). IslamicFinder. https://www.islamicfinder.org/news/5-spiritual-impacts-of-Salah-in-our-daily-lives/

5 verses from the Qur'an that remind us to be thankful. (2017, November 22). Muslim Girl. https://muslimgirl.com/5-verses-quran-remind-us-thankful/

5 ways to find the Qibla for prayer. (2007, April 28). WikiHow. https://www.wikihow.com/Find-the-Qibla-for-Prayer

9 everyday duas that Muslim parents should teach their kids. (2020, June 20). The Islamic Quotes - Islamic Status - Islamic Forum | Islamic Quotes About Everything. https://www.theislamicquotes.com/duas-muslim-parents-should-teach-their-kids/

Abdulla, A. (2019, September 3). Assalamualaikum Warahmatullahi Wabarakatuh (rewards of saying). My Islam. https://myislam.org/assalamualaikum-warahmatullahi-wabarakatuh/

Abdulla, A. (2020, April 9). 67+ verses in Quran about Salah (prayer quotes). My Islam. https://myislam.org/verses-in-quran-about-Salah/

Abdulla, A. (2020, March 25). What is the tashahhud Dua for Salah? (when to say). My Islam. https://myislam.org/tashahhud-dua-for-salah/

Ahmed, I. (2021, January 6). Spiritual benefits of prayer. The Siasat Daily. https://www.siasat.com/spiritual-benefits-of-prayer-2061568/

Aisha Stacey (© 2013IslamReligion.com). (n.d.). The Wisdom behind the Postures and Phrases of Prayer (part 1 of 2): Can certain positions really bring a person closer to God? Islamreligion.com. https://www.islamreligion.com/articles/10272/wisdom-behind-postures-and-phrases-of-prayer-part-1/

Al Ahmed, A. (2019, December 25). Dua before and after eating. Kiflayn; Kiflayn.com. https://kiflayn.com/duaas-before-and-after-eating/

Ali, H. (2017, February 17). 10 Benefits of Performing Wudu according to Hadith. Prayer Time NYC. https://www.prayertimenyc.com/performing-Wudu-benefits/

Ali, Z. (2019, February 21). The Duas of the prophets and the pious. Zakeeya Ali. https://www.zakeeyaali.com/blog/duas-of-the-prophets-and-the-pious

Alkurdi, Z. (2019, June 3). 9 practical tips for developing a prayer habit - Zeena alkurdi. Medium. https://medium.com/@zeenakurdi/9-practical-tips-to-developing-a-prayer-habit-8b613f42ccc9

Ansari, A. (2020, February 18). 40 important supplications/duas for kids | Quran For kids. Quran For Kids.

Ansari, A. (2020, July 18). The Concept of Worship of Allah in Islam | Quran For kids. Quran For Kids.

Ayah al-baqarah (the cow) 2:34. (n.d.). Islamawakened.com. https://www.islamawakened.com/quran/2/34/

Ballam, R. (n.d.). Wudu in 10 simple steps! Aliandsumaya.com. https://aliandsumaya.com/Wudu10steps/

Bharakda, A. (2022, February 8). 16 practical tips to stay focused during prayer. Themuslimvibe.com; The Muslim Vibe. https://themuslimvibe.com/faith-islam/17-practical-tips-to-stay-focused-during-prayer

Breathing techniques for stress relief. (n.d.). WebMD. https://www.webmd.com/balance/stress-management/stress-relief-breathing-techniques

Call to prayers (adhaan) - sunnah.com - sayings and teachings of prophet Muhammad (صلى الله عليه و سلم). (n.d.). Sunnah.com. https://sunnah.com/bukhari/10

Call to prayers (adhaan). (n.d.). Edu.My. https://www.iium.edu.my/deed/hadith/bukhari/011_sbt.html

Children! Let's listen to a blessed hadees - Salah and children. (2019, August 20). Dawateislami.net; I.T Majlis. https://www.dawateislami.net/magazine/en/bachon-ka-mahnama/importance-of-Salah-for-kids

Du'a before and after eating (4 du'as). (2023, June 6). My Islam. https://myislam.org/dua-before-eating-and-dua-after-eating/

Du'a for any mode of transportation. (2023, June 6). My Islam. https://myislam.org/dua-for-any-mode-of-transportation/

Dua' for Increase in Knowledge – Compiled and translated By Abbas Abu Yahya. (2013, July 18). Abdurrahman.org. https://abdurrahman.org/2013/07/18/dua-for-increase-in-knowledge-compiled-and-translated-by-abbas-abu-yahya/

Dudley Industries. (2020, February 6). About Wudu - Questions on Wudu answered. Dudleyindustries.com. https://www.dudleyindustries.com/news/about-Wudu-questions-on-Wudu-answered

Elias, A. A. (2017, February 19). Hadith on Salat: Praying the five prayers saves from Hellfire. Daily Hadith Online. https://www.abuaminaelias.com/dailyhadithonline/2017/02/19/salawat-khams-save-nar/

en-asks. (2022, October 25). Times of the five daily prayers. Home; اسلام اون لاین. https://fiqh.islamonline.net/en/times-of-the-five-daily-prayers/

Firdous, N. (n.d.). Everything you need to know about the Qibla. Quran Academy. https://quranacademy.io/blog/everything-need-know-Qibla/

Fouzia, M. (2019, December 27). The Prophet Muhammad's favorite perfume. About Islam. https://aboutislam.net/reading-islam/about-muhammad/the-prophet-muhammads-favorite-perfume/

Habeeba. (2013, August 1). When in salaat: 8 ways to increase focus during prayer. Muslim Girl. https://muslimgirl.com/when-in-salaat/

Hadith: The reward of repeating after the Adhan (prayer call). (n.d.). Encyclopedia of Translated Prophetic Hadiths. https://hadeethenc.com/en/browse/hadith/65086

Hagi-Aden, I. (2016, October 31). Chapter 1 - what is Salah and why do we pray? - masjid ar-Rahmah. Masjid Ar-Rahmah | Mosque of Mercy; Masjid ar-Rahmah. https://www.mymasjid.ca/beginners-guide-learn-pray-Salah/chapter-1/

Hagi-Aden, I. (2016, October 31). Chapter 2 - how to make Wudu, step by step - masjid ar-Rahmah. Masjid Ar-Rahmah | Mosque of Mercy; Masjid ar-Rahmah. https://www.mymasjid.ca/beginners-guide-learn-pray-Salah/chapter-2/

Hagi-Aden, I. (2016, October 31). Chapter 4 - how to pray Salah, step by step - masjid ar-Rahmah. Masjid Ar-Rahmah | Mosque of Mercy; Masjid ar-Rahmah. https://www.mymasjid.ca/beginners-guide-learn-pray-salah/chapter-4/

HalalTrip. (n.d.). Adhan: The Call for Prayers (Transliteration). HalalTrip. https://www.halaltrip.com/other/blog/Adhan-transliteration/

Hameed, S. (2023, February 24). Why was the Qiblah changed from Jerusalem to Makkah? About Islam. https://aboutislam.net/reading-islam/understanding-islam/why-was-the-Qiblah-changed-from-jerusalem-to-makkah/

Hands, M. (2019, March 28). The five daily prayer times and why we observe them. Org.uk. https://muslimhands.org.uk/latest/2019/03/the-five-daily-prayer-times-and-why-we-observe-them

History of Qibla: The shift from Bait-ul Maqdas to Masjid-al Haram. (n.d.). IslamicFinder. https://www.islamicfinder.org/news/history-of-Qibla-the-shift-from-bait-ul-maqdas-to-masjid-al-haram/

How to find Qibla direction with compass? (n.d.). Qiblafinder.org. https://www.Qiblafinder.org/how-to-find-Qibla-direction-with-compass.html

How to make Dhikr and Dua a daily habit. (2018, April 1). AYEINA. https://ayeina.com/make-dhikr-a-daily-habit/

How to perform wudhu – A step-by-step guide for beginners. (n.d.). Muslim.Sg. https://muslim.sg/articles/how-to-perform-wudhu-a-step-by-step-guide-for-beginners

Huda. (2004, May 19). What does the Adhan (Islamic call to prayer) mean? Learn Religions. https://www.learnreligions.com/what-do-the-words-of-the-Adhan-mean-in-english-2003812

Hudda, A. (2018, September 21). Importance of Salat in its Prime Time (Awwal al-Waqt). Al-islam.org. https://www.al-islam.org/articles/importance-salat-its-prime-time-awwal-al-waqt-arifa-hudda

Humayun, S. (2022, March 25). How to find peace through prayer? 3 powerful triggers. About Islam. https://aboutislam.net/spirituality/how-to-find-peace-through-prayer-3-powerful-triggers/

Ilm, P. (2021, September 6). Salah for Kids: Teaching kids how to pray. Primary Ilm. https://primaryilm.com/Salah-for-kids-teaching-kids-how-to-pray/

Ilm, P. (2023, May 14). Wudhu steps. Primary Ilm. https://primaryilm.com/wudhu-steps/

Iman. (2023, February 8). Hayya Alal falah and Hayya Alal Salah in Arabic and meaning. Imanupdate.com. https://imanupdate.com/hayya-alal-falah/

Importance of cleanliness in Islam. (2018a, February 13). Islamic Articles. https://www.quranreading.com/blog/importance-of-cleanliness-in-islam-quranic-verses-and-ahadith-on-purity/

Importance of cleanliness in Islam. (2018b, October 24). Qamar Islam Khan; admin. https://qamarislamkhan.com/importance-of-cleanliness-in-islam/

Importance of making Dua. (2021, September 7). Islam The Ultimate Peace - Islam The Ultimate Peace. https://islamtheultimatepeace.com/importance-of-making-dua/

Iqamat (Iqamah). (n.d.). Islam Ahmadiyya. https://www.alislam.org/book/salat/Iqamah/

Islam. (n.d.). Islam - Children's Corner. Worldofislam.Info. https://special.worldofislam.info/index.php?page=Children/Stories/The%20Story%20of%20Adhan

IslamicFinder. (n.d.-a). Duas After leaving toilet. IslamicFinder. https://www.islamicfinder.org/duas/masnoon/after-leaving-toilet/

IslamicFinder. (n.d.-b). Duas Before entering toilet. IslamicFinder. https://www.islamicfinder.org/duas/masnoon/before-entering-toilet/

IslamicFinder. (n.d.-c). Duas before sleeping. IslamicFinder. https://www.islamicfinder.org/duas/masnoon/before-sleeping/

IslamicFinder. (n.d.-d). Duas when leaving home. IslamicFinder. https://www.islamicfinder.org/duas/masnoon/when-leaving-home/

IslamicFinder. (n.d.-e). Duas when waking up. IslamicFinder. https://www.islamicfinder.org/duas/masnoon/when-waking-up/

IslamicFinder. (n.d.-f). Duas when wearing a garment. IslamicFinder. https://www.islamicfinder.org/duas/masnoon/when-wearing-a-garment/

islamonline_en. (2021, November 5). The Adhan (the call to prayer). IslamOnline. https://islamonline.net/en/the-Adhan-the-call-to-prayer/

It is not permissible to prostrate to anyone other than Allah, even if it is only by way of veneration and showing respect. (n.d.). Islamqa.Info. https://islamqa.info/en/answers/211400/it-is-not-permissible-to-prostrate-to-anyone-other-than-allah-even-if-it-is-only-by-way-of-veneration-and-showing-respect

Meehan, S. (2023, April 13). 4 spiritual benefits prayer grants you. About Islam. https://aboutislam.net/spirituality/4-spiritual-benefits-that-prayer-grants-you/

Meehan, S. (2023, April 13). 4 spiritual benefits prayer grants you. About Islam. https://aboutislam.net/spirituality/4-spiritual-benefits-that-prayer-grants-you/

Mohammad, M. S. (2023, January 6). Importance of Salah in Islam {with hadith references}. IslamKaZikr. https://islamkazikr.com/importance-of-Salah/

Motala, M. S. (n.d.). The du'a after drinking milk – Hadith Answers. Hadithanswers.com. https://hadithanswers.com/the-dua-after-drinking-milk/

Musofer, M. A. (2012, September 28). Importance of cleanliness. Dawn. https://www.dawn.com/news/752560/importance-of-cleanliness

Najimi, S. (2022, August 8). What is the difference between Athan and Iqamah? Masjidal. https://mymasjidal.com/blogs/history/what-is-the-difference-between-athan-and-iqaamah

Postures of Muslim prayer explained. (2020, March 3). About Islam. https://aboutislam.net/reading-islam/understanding-islam/postures-of-muslim-prayer-explained/

Prayer. (n.d.). BBC. https://www.bbc.co.uk/bitesize/guides/zhnhsrd/revision/3

Quranic Reflection No. 436. Āyat 2:208 – Submission to Allah 'azaa wajall. (2019, September 9). The Academy for Learning Islam. https://academyofislam.com/quranic-reflection-no-436-ayat-2208-submission-to-allah-azaa-wajall/

Responding to the Adhan. (n.d.). Life With Allah. https://lifewithallah.com/articles/other/act-upon-the-etiquettes-of-the-masjid-and-respond-to-the-Adhan-2/

RNZ News. (2019, March 22). What is the call to prayer? RNZ. https://www.rnz.co.nz/news/national/385330/what-is-the-call-to-prayer

SAHIH MUSLIM, BOOK 4: The book of prayers (kitab Al-Salat)(part I). (n.d.). Edu.My. https://www.iium.edu.my/deed/hadith/muslim/004_smt.html

Samina. (2020, August 24). How to help kids love Salah (list of motivational verses and ahadith on prayer). AYEINA. https://ayeina.com/kids-love-Salah-motivational-verses-ahadith/

Samina. (2020, August 24). How to help kids love Salah (list of motivational verses and ahadith on prayer). AYEINA. https://ayeina.com/kids-love-salah-motivational-verses-ahadith/

Significance of the change of Qiblah. (2014, September 20). Islamway.net; Islamway. https://en.islamway.net/article/30775/significance-of-the-change-of-Qiblah

So high [above all] is Allah, the Sovereign, the Truth. And, [O. (n.d.). Surahquran.com. https://surahquran.com/english-aya-114-sora-20.html

Sofuoglu, M. (2022, May 10). What makes Adhan (Azaan) so important for Muslims? TRT WORLD. https://www.trtworld.com/magazine/what-makes-Adhan-azaan-so-important-for-muslims-57019

Spiritual benefits of Prayer. (2014, July 20). Facts about the Muslims & the Religion of Islam - Toll-Free Hotline 1-877-WHY-ISLAM. https://www.whyislam.org/spiritual-benefits-of-prayer/

Stacey, A. (2023, April 9). The wisdom behind the postures and phrases of prayer. About Islam. https://aboutislam.net/spirituality/whats-the-wisdom-behind-the-postures-and-phrases-of-prayer/

Strategies for concentrating in prayer. (2021, November 8). Al-islam.org. https://www.al-islam.org/concentration-prayer-jameel-kermalli/strategies-concentrating-prayer

Super User. (n.d.). Adhan and Iqamah (for kids and teens). Mohammadfnd.org. https://mohammadfnd.org/en/kids-and-teens/islamic-laws-fiqh/636-Adhan-and-Iqamah-for-kids-and-teens

Super User. (n.d.). Cleanliness in Islam. Spiritofislam.Co.In. https://spiritofislam.co.in/spiritnew/index.php/cleanliness-in-islam

Surah Al-baqarah - 144. (n.d.). Quran.com. https://quran.com/2/144?translations=17,21,22,31,84,85,95,101

Surah Ali 'Imran - 96. (n.d.). Quran.com. https://quran.com/en/ali-imran/96

Surah Al-ma'idah - 6. (n.d.). Quran.com. https://quran.com/5:6?font=v1&translations=149%2C131%2C84%2C17%2C85%2C95%2C19%2C22

Tawfiq, A. I. (2022, February 3). What are the Benefits of Five Daily Prayers? About Islam. https://aboutislam.net/counseling/ask-about-islam/what-are-the-benefits-of-the-five-daily-prayers/

Teach your children How To Pray Salah at right age. (n.d.). Getsajdah.com. https://getsajdah.com/blog/teach-your-children-how-to-pray-Salah-at-right-age

The Editors of Encyclopedia Britannica. (2023). Qiblah. In Encyclopedia Britannica.

The importance and significance of Adhan in Islam. (2018, October 10). Islamic Articles. https://www.quranreading.com/blog/the-importance-and-significance-of-Adhan-in-islam/

The meaning of worship and submission in Islam. (2013, February 9). SeekersGuidance. https://seekersguidance.org/answers/general-counsel/the-meaning-of-worship-and-submission-in-islam/

The Pen. (n.d.). What do the movements in the prayer mean? Thepenmagazine.net. https://thepenmagazine.net/what-do-the-movements-in-the-prayer-mean/

The Pen. (n.d.). What do the movements in the prayer mean? Thepenmagazine.net. https://thepenmagazine.net/what-do-the-movements-in-the-prayer-mean/

The psychological and social importance of postures during worship. (n.d.). Spsp.org. https://spsp.org/news-center/character-context-blog/psychological-and-social-importance-postures-during-worship

The Quranic Arabic Corpus - Translation. (n.d.). Quran.com. https://corpus.quran.com/translation.jsp?chapter=11&verse=114

Value and Importance of Dua in Islam. (2017, December 21). Islamic Articles. https://www.quranreading.com/blog/value-and-importance-of-dua-in-islam/

Wahab, A. (2014, September 18). Importance of Salah (prayer) according to the holy Quran. Islamic Articles. https://www.quranreading.com/blog/importance-of-Salah-prayer-according-to-the-holy-quran/

Was the Adhan revealed by wahy or was it suggested by a sahaabi? - Islam Question & Answer. (n.d.). Islamqa.Info. https://islamqa.info/en/answers/7945/was-the-Adhan-revealed-by-wahy-or-was-it-suggested-by-a-sahaabi

What is Islam? (2014, November 17). Facts about the Muslims & the Religion of Islam - Toll-Free Hotline 1-877-WHY-ISLAM. https://www.whyislam.org/what-is-submission/

What is the meaning of the angels prostrating to Adam and Yoosuf's brothers prostrating to him? - Islam Question & Answer. (n.d.). Islamqa.Info. https://islamqa.info/en/answers/8492/what-is-the-meaning-of-the-angels-prostrating-to-adam-and-yoosufs-brothers-prostrating-to-him

What to say upon hearing the Adhan? 5 things. (2016, December 25). About Islam. https://aboutislam.net/reading-islam/finding-peace/remembering-allah/what-to-say-upon-hearing-the-Adhan-5-things/

Why should prayer be a vital part of your child's everyday routine? (2019, August 26). Gurukul. https://gurukultheschool.com/blog/why-should-prayer-be-a-vital-part-of-your-childs-everyday-routine/

Wudu steps - How to Perform Wudu or Ablution? | Quran For kids. (2020, January 14). Quran For Kids.

2022) .إ, أحمد, December 18). Significance of prayer. IslamOnline. https://islamonline.net/en/significance-of-prayer

Made in the USA
Las Vegas, NV
10 June 2024

90951048R00050